For my Father, Dad (some people called him Larry). You helped me set my first goals and even though I didn't get enough time with you to allow you to see me truly achieving the big ones... I think you know.

THE GOALS *Journal*
..... If it's here, it happens ....

DUANE ALLEY

Duane Alley
TRAINING

Copyright © 2015 by Duane Alley – http://www.duanealley.com

All rights reserved. No part of this book may be produced or utilised in any form or by any means, electronic or mechanical, including photocopying, recording or by any information storage and retrieval system, without permission in writing from the Publisher.

Published 2015

Publisher: Performance Results Pty Ltd t/as Performance Results Publishing

Graphic Design & Layout: Mélissa Caron – Go-Enki.com
Editor: Richard Burian – Richard-Burian.com

Self Help

ISBN 978-0-9870571-8-1

— TABLE OF CONTENTS —

INTRODUCTION: GOAL SETTING IN GENERAL 9

- *The Goals Journal* Story 11

- Making It More Powerful 12

- Visualisation 13

- Reward 17

- V for Victory 19

- Values 20

- Saying It Better 22

- Final Words 25

INSTRUCTIONS: HOW TO USE *THE GOALS JOURNAL* 27

GOALS JOURNAL PAGES 31

ABOUT THE AUTHOR: DUANE ALLEY 234

introduction
GOAL SETTING IN GENERAL

introduction :
— GOAL SETTING IN GENERAL —

— THE GOALS JOURNAL STORY —

Years ago, I was running a Presentation Skills Training in LA for a few hundred people and I had a guest drop in. Mark Victor Hansen, co-creator of the *Chicken Soup For The Soul* books (among many other things) spent a few hours at the Training catching up, talking with the audience and generally being an incredibly inspiring man – as he always is. As we were talking, he told me a story of how he kept a journal with all his goals in it and had done so for years. In fact, he'd always chosen to write down the goals and carry the journal with him so he could constantly remind himself of his vision and desired achievements. He had over 1,000 goals in his journals that he'd been adding to since before his first books came out. And he said he'd finally met someone with as many goals as he had.

He'd been speaking at an event in Las Vegas and another speaker and he had started a conversation about goals. During that conversation the other speaker, Dr John Demartini, mentioned he also kept a journal for goals and had over 1,000 goals. They both took out their journals and shared. This started a tradition for them of getting together when they could and sharing goals and victories. For me, it sparked my excitement.

I had goals lists, for sure. I knew that writing down goals gave them a whole new level of pending reality that didn't happen if they were just 'in my head'. So I went out and bought a new journal just for the purpose of writing down my goals. Collecting all the lists I'd made to add to the journal was fun (and time consuming) and totally worth it, because I had a place to put all the goals I'd been setting and somewhere to add future ones.

— Making It More Powerful —

Having all my goals in a journal was fantastic. I carried it with me as I was traveling all over the world running live trainings and for holidays. It sat on my desk at the Office when I was working and lived in my bedside table at night.

One day, sitting on a beach in Portugal, adding a new goal to the journal I got thinking. See, I'd just finished teaching a solid week of powerful success and achievement strategies to 400+ incredible and entrepreneurially minded participants, drilling them on the power and importance of their dreams and goals; guiding them in putting more effort and attention into how they set their goals and the power behind their purpose in wanting their goals. We had talked about Neville and his incredible book, *The Power of Awareness* and how he instructed his readers to 'imagine the moment of the wish fulfilled', visioning their goals within themselves. He called it 'believing it in'. There was more we could do to make our dreams, wishes, wants and desires a reality than just set a goal and hope it would happen.

Then it hit me that I'd just been writing a list. Like a grocery list but for goals. If these really were the things I wanted to create in my life, then they deserved more respect than just being a part of a list. What if I could add all the other study I'd done with achievement experts, modelling of masters of success and processes I'd created with the *Science of Change* Trainings?

This was the true start of *The Goals Journal*. Bringing together a number of the most powerful elements of goal achievement and the psychology of success. It is something that I have continued to work on over the years and released in a limited form during some of my live training events. Now is the time to share it with others to make a massive difference to your goal achievement so that you can continue to build your future and own your life.

The most powerful distinction I made straight away was the use of...

— VISUALISATION —

Peak performance athletes and mystics alike have known a secret that has helped them achieve greatness for themselves and others. The power of visualising the achievement of their goals. All visualising is imagining pictures of what you want. Most people visualise internally, that is they see the picture (or imagine/pretend seeing the picture) inside their own mind. When I was studying Neville and *The Power of Awareness* I learnt that first I must believe the achievement inside me and then 'out-picture' it so that I could live into the dream, goal or wish fulfilled.

This is talking about the power of vision boards or other external visioning techniques. These processes are popular now from personal development classes through to boardrooms. It's the same process behind building a model of a cathedral before it's built, to generals mapping out a battle plan with little pretend soldiers on a mock table top countryside. It's about physically seeing the achievement before it is created in the (full scale) real world.

By externally visualising, we are creating an inspirational image that we can latch onto and focus our efforts to achieve. All goals are first created visually on an internal level; we imagine the creation of the desired object or event. Then most people go to work attempting to make it so. When we get into visualising the achievement externally, we create a second level of power boost to our efforts. This gives us something to focus on so that we can truly employ Neville's technique of 'imagining the moment of the wish fulfilled', believing in its achievement and our success.

I have taught participants and coached business people to use vision boards, but only for short-term goals. Many years ago I had a friend who moved apartments in San Francisco. She was a very big vision board person and had her main ones on her lounge room wall. She'd also lived in the same apartment for a number of years. I was speaking with her a few months after she'd moved and asked her where she had put her vision boards in the new place. A look of shock came over her face, and then she laughed. She'd forgotten all about them till that moment. They must still be, she said, hanging on the wall of the old apartment. See, they'd become so much part of 'the furniture' that they literally disappeared for her. She didn't see them when she was packing and just left them behind.

Vision boards, when hung for a long time, can just disappear out of our conscious awareness. Yes, the subconscious mind will continue to take in the image and embed them at a deep level, but consciously they do nothing. And it's the conscious focus on the desire added to the unconscious emotion you will attach to achieving it that will drive your true success. One without the other is nowhere near as strong.

My recommendation for anyone creating a set of longer-term goals is to put them in a book. No one ever opens a book without a conscious intention. And what you want when you are visualising goals is a conscious intention – you want to use the power of visualisation to help you achieve the goals.

Knowing this, it was critical that a visualising page must be included in *The Goals Journal*. You start by writing down the goal in as few words as possible at the top of the right hand page (where it says 'Goal'). Feel free to flick forward to a full journal page and have a look so you can really see what I am talking about and know what to do when it's your turn.

Don't worry about how you state the goal at the moment, that's going to come later at a more appropriate and effective time. There are more spaces on the right hand side page, under your goal, and you will fill these in as well. I will explain what they are all for. Now I want you to start collecting images that will be stuck into the left hand side page, opposite the words about your goal. This is the visualising page.

You want to select images that inspire you to think of the goal and of the emotion you will feel when you finally achieve your desire. Feel free to draw, sketch or add whatever kind of imagery will work for you. And, cutting out and gluing in pictures is absolutely okay for some more artistically challenged (like me). I also encourage you to use a few inspirational words or phrases if you come across them as they help. Take up the whole page or just use a few images that really hit home for you. I don't mind; this is your goals journal and your goal.

People sometimes ask me about people in the images. What if they want to get married and they are pasting a picture of a man or woman ('of their dreams'), but they actually probably don't really want to marry the model in the photo. Will that make a problem? The answer is no. You are using images that inspire you and most importantly represent the desired outcome or wish fulfilled. The images themselves are not going to magically come alive and change your future... usually. Although I do caution you to be specific in what the content of your images are.

One Member who has completed many training programs with me over a number of years often shares this story. Her name is Tania and during one of our *Lockdown Retreats* (a program designed to help you craft the year ahead to be the best year of your life; by systematically discovering the biggest achievements you want to make and then creating a plan to get there) was working on her vision board. We use boards at Lockdown as the visioned goals are only for the next 12 months.

Tania wanted to create a relationship and found the perfect picture and stuck it dead centre in her masterpiece. About 18 months later, when she returned to the program, she warned the rest of the Members to be aware and specific. She was initially only wanting to create a relationship and had thought she'd found a beautiful image of a woman who looked a little like her and a man who she could imagine represented her new and as yet unfound beau. What she had failed to notice was that they were both wearing wedding rings and were actually watching their little girl play in a playground in the background of the picture.

You've probably guessed what happened, right? And you'd be correct. Within a month of the board creation Tania had met an incredible man and the relationship had swept them both off their feet and into their wedding. As she told the story, she and Hayden (the new relationship turned new husband) were expecting the birth of their first child... a daughter. Tania's words of wisdom, 'Be inspired by the pictures and be careful what they actually are.' Very similar to that age-old parental guidance to 'be careful what you wish for because you may get it'. By the way, Tania and Hayden is a story of amazing creation – they are deeply in love and have a gorgeous little baby girl. This is definitely not a cautionary tale, but something you want to take note of.

— Reward —

One of the key elements and core truths that we teach in our programs is that for every achievement there needs to be a reward.

So many people set goals, then stress about getting them. Then eventually, when they actually achieve them, there is a release of that stress. And guess what happens next...? They immediately set a brand-new goal. Do you know anyone like this? Do you know them very well?

This kind of stress and release cycle, which we've all done before, creates a shift in our psychology and a very negative reaction in our neurochemistry, which causes a flood through your brain of the neurochemicals responsible for aggression, agitation and stress. In fact, setting goals then stressing to get a goal and then getting a goal and having that release of stress and then immediately setting another goal is one of the most common reasons why many people don't achieve goals in their life, in their business or in their relationships, health, wealth or any other area of their lives. There is a way to stop this. And it's with the addition of a single very important point, a pause. I suggest to people that when they set a goal they're going to stress about getting that goal and that's a natural reaction and occurrence. But then when they achieve the goal and release that stress, it's important for them to pause and rest. At that point they want to look back and review what they've achieved and then reward themselves for the achievement of that goal. This not only shifts the psychology and neurochemistry around goal setting, getting and achievement, it also helps to build and validate the belief that what you have achieved has value and worth enough to be rewarded.

Then when you set a new goal, at the same time, set the reward that they can look forward to on the achievement of a goal. This rest, review and reward process sets up a very different psychological and neurochemical cycle inside of the brain. The different chemicals that are released during this cycle lead to a general feeling of well being as well as a feeling of rest, comfort and happiness. These neurochemicals are very addictive by nature and cause you to become addicted to the rewards that you receive from achieving your goals. Your unconscious mind begins to associate very quickly the achievement reward and the good feelings it gets from the new neurochemical cycle to the achievement of goals and it helps you achieve those goals so that you can get more rewards.

To really make this work, what is critical is that we associate the reward that we are allowing ourselves to receive with the achievement of the goal that we set out. It's also pretty important to make sure that the reward is relative to the achievement. I mean, if your goal is to sketch out the first page of the new website and you do that today, then take yourself on a week-long all-expenses-paid vacation to Paris or Las Vegas (or both), it's a little bit over kill. Similarly, if you achieve one of the biggest projects of your life and then only take yourself down the road for a quick chai latte, it's going to be a little bit under doing the reward. It's important to remember to keep the reward relative and to remember that rewards can range from low cost, to no cost whatsoever, to something more expensive.

When it comes to *The Goals Journal* we implement this strategy straight away. After we write about our initial short version of the goal, using the least words possible to describe the achievement we want, we then immediately set the reward that will give us or allow ourselves to have the achievement of this goal.

— V for Victory —

One of the pieces that I really loved hearing from Mark when he first explained how he used his goals journal was the fact that instead of just ticking off the goal, crossing it out, or highlighting in some way to represent his completion of that goal, he did something very special. He put a large 'V' over the goal to represent victory in his life after having achieved something that he set out to do. I love this idea and from that moment on, every goal achievement I started marking with a 'V for Victory'.

You'll notice on *The Goals Journal* right hand side pages a space for you to check off the achievement of each of your goals with a 'V' if you wish. Let this be the reminder that you have created a victory for yourself and it's time for reward and celebration in your life for achieving this goal.

— Values —

Our values are a very important set of beliefs of what is most important to us at any moment in time. Being such, values provide upfront motivation for all action and the focal point and driving force behind achieving any goal. In fact, they are the reason that we set goals in the first place. We set goals in order for us to achieve our values. Let me explain...

Many people think of goals and outcomes as being synonyms (different words with the same meaning). I don't necessarily agree with this. I think goals are the events that have to occur or are necessary so that once achieved, will lead you to a desired state. This state is what I call the outcome. It's literally what comes out of you achieving your goals.

If I was to ask anyone in any western or westernised country if they wanted to be rich, the majority of people will answer with a resounding, 'yes'. When asked how rich they want to be, the most commonly given answer is 'a millionaire'. When those same people are asked what 'millionaire' means, they don't give an economic definition. Instead, they would give what I call 'lifestyle symptomology'. They would say that they wanted their life to be one of freedom, to be able to send their children to the school of their choosing, to be able to travel anywhere any time by any means they want, to be able to afford the health or lifestyle that they choose... The list goes on.

This lifestyle symptomology is not about being 'a millionaire' (which has a distinct economic definition). What it is instead, is what they imagine the life or lifestyle that being a millionaire would create. Becoming a millionaire is the goal. But the lifestyle is the outcome.

Our outcome is the living of our values.

If one of your highest values were freedom, for example, then the goals that you set would be goals that you believe would lead you to a place of freedom. If on the other hand, you valued wealth as a higher value, then all the goals you set with the goals that you believe when achieved would create wealth for you. The same is true if your values are love, or if you value health, or if one your values is family. Whatever our highest values are is what we're going to be focusing on in setting our goals and therefore our achievements. This happens at a very subconscious level. We don't generally consciously think of our values before we set the goals. We're going to take control of that in *The Goals Journal*.

It's critical then, in *The Goals Journal* and when setting goals at any time for us to be aware of what the driving values are behind the achievement of that goal. We do this simply by asking ourselves when we achieve the desire, dream, wish, win or goal how we will feel. What positive emotions will this achievement win for us in our life? Succeeding in this way, what will this deliver or give to us? Values are usually single words or short word phrases (that means one to three words). Values are also generally emotional states or closely related to other emotional states.

Usually, when I'm working with people and setting goals or setting my own goals, I make sure that I have a minimum of one, but a maximum of three values associated with the achievement of any of the goals. Of course there will be other things that are important to you, but we're really looking for the most critical and the most important values that will be filled by the achievement of this goal. Keeping it down between one and three allows us to work on something that is workable.

— Saying It Better —

Now that you've got all these pieces of your goal setting in place it's important to begin speaking about it or stating it in such a way that it causes a subconscious programming of the success. What usually happens when people talk about their goals is they say them in such a way to prove they actually don't have it. For example, people will say, 'I want to have a holiday on a tropical island'.

What they are really doing is telling their subconscious mind they don't currently have a holiday and that they just want it. The subconscious mind will continue to deliver on the exact input it is given. When you tell it that you 'don't have a holiday, but want one,' it will continue to deliver you 'not having a holiday, but wanting one'.

The only way to overcome this and to use the natural function of your subconscious mind is to state the future desired goal in such a way that the subconscious hears it as a present fact and can then operate on proving your assumption or belief as real. That means helping you get it.

By doing this it also creates a specific psychology around the imagining of our goal. Achievements experts have a name for this; we call it 'Structural Tension'. It means the subconscious is being programmed to believe you have something and at the same time the conscious mind is aware of the opposite and knows you don't. This tension can only be resolved by the achievement of the goal. This means the power of your subconscious faculties will work even harder and in alignment with your conscious focus to achieve the outcome as you desire.

So here's how to do it...

The first thing you need to discover is what has to happen in order to prove to you that you have achieved your goal. You need to know what evidence your conscious mind needs to see here or feel in order to believe the goal is achieved. We call this the 'evidence procedure' and 'end step'.

First we start by stating the goal achievement date in the present and positive. You put in whatever day and date you're setting as your goal achievement moment.

> Example:
> 'It is now May 12, 2016'

Then you add what I call your emotional hook space that is the emotion you will feel when you achieve this thing you want. As emotions can only be felt in the present moment (that is, you can't feel excited soon, you can only feel excited when you feel excited), this emotional state creates a beacon for your subconscious mind to latch onto and helps focusing in on the present moment and imagining your experience in the future.

> Example:
> 'It is now May 12, 2016 and I am feeling excited...'

Third, it's now time to state the end step/evidence procedure for your achievement.

> Example:
> It is now May 12, 2016 and I feel excited;
> I am walking through the entrance to Club Med;
> I have arrived to join The Inner Game of Everything *experience with inspirational people*

The basic structure is:

STATED GOAL

It is now _May 12, 2016_

I feel _excited_

I am _walking through the entrance to Club Med_

I have _arrived to join The Inner Game of Everything experience with inspirational people_

— Final Words —

I'm so excited about sharing *The Goals Journal* with you now. This is something that I never shared outside of specific Live Training events before. It's a different way of thinking, a different way of feeling into your goals. And I'm sure that you know now this is a different way of helping you achieve your goals and successes and a higher level.

It's time for you to get into this journal now. Begin using it in the way I described above and find new creative and interesting ways to empower your goals and to power your achievement more and better than ever before. Start using *The Goals Journal* to help you build your future and own your life.

And please share your achievements with as many people as possible and with me; I'd love to hear about your own personal achievements that come out of you using *The Goals Journal*. Remember you cannot be inspiring unless you're first inspired so continue to do that to people.

Green lights and let's get going...

·········· instructions ··········

HOW TO USE THE GOALS JOURNAL

instructions :
— HOW TO USE *THE GOALS JOURNAL* —

Ok, so you're just about ready to start.

Let's just review how to use the *Journal* to get the best out of it. First up, there's no best way; there's what I suggest here and then there's how you adapt that to work best for you. The true test will be your increasing ability to really feel into the getting of your goals and how you more easily and effortlessly achieve what you put down in these pages.

First up, if you have other goals written down in other places, gather all those together and transfer them into *The Goals Journal*. You will have one place with all your important goals and can carry this with you to review and claim victory as you work, play, love and live your life.

The first thing to do is just to write down your goal in the least number of words possible... easy. Don't worry about fancy language at this time; just say it simple and the way you want it.

Remember, as soon as you set a goal out there for yourself, you want to set up the reward too. So, that's your next step: what are you going to do and how are you going to reward the achievement of this goal when done?

When you do achieve this goal it will fulfil some of your most important and powerful driving values. That is, the things you believe are most important to you. Take some time to truly understand why this goal is important to you and list the most important value (between one to three) in the Values section.

Now – time to state the goal in the most powerful 'Future Stated' method. Refer back to how I told you this works a couple of pages ago till you've got it down on automatic.

With all the writing done on the right hand side page, it's time to really get into visualising on the left hand side page.

Find pictures, inspirations, imagines, phrases, and words or just draw them in yourself. Online, magazines, brochures… there are so many sources available to craft this visioning page. And the cool news is that you can add to it at any time.

After you have this down, it's time to take some time. Imagine the achievement of the goal on or before the date you chose and allow yourself the feeling of the wish fulfilled. Immerse yourself in that for a time so you can really let your subconscious mind soak it in.

Then the most important thing of all – get out there and start making it happen. Remember, action is the first missing ingredient to success and nothing worth having isn't worth doing to get.

That's it – go get 'em!

...... if it's here, it happens ......

GOALS JOURNAL

START DATE :

IMAGES of Goal and Achievement

GOAL

VICTORY
☐
ACHIEVED

REWARDS

VALUES Fulfilled by Achievement

STATED GOAL

It is now

I feel

I am

I have

IMAGES of Goal and Achievement

Goal

VICTORY ☐ ACHIEVED

Rewards

Values Fulfilled by Achievement

Stated Goal

It is now _____

I feel _____

I am _____

I have _____

IMAGES of Goal and Achievement

Goal

VICTORY ☐ ACHIEVED

Rewards

Values Fulfilled by Achievement

Stated Goal

It is now _____

I feel _____

I am _____

I have _____

IMAGES of Goal and Achievement

GOAL

VICTORY ☐ ACHIEVED

REWARDS

VALUES Fulfilled by Achievement

STATED GOAL

It is now

I feel

I am

I have

IMAGES of Goal and Achievement

Goal

VICTORY ☐ ACHIEVED

Rewards

Values Fulfilled by Achievement

Stated Goal

It is now _____

I feel _____
_____

I am _____
_____
_____

I have _____
_____

IMAGES of Goal and Achievement

Goal

Victory Achieved ☐

Rewards

Values Fulfilled by Achievement

Stated Goal

It is now _____

I feel _____
_____

I am _____
_____
_____

I have _____
_____

IMAGES of Goal and Achievement

Goal

VICTORY
☐
ACHIEVED

Rewards

Values Fulfilled by Achievement

Stated Goal

It is now _____

I feel _____
_____

I am _____
_____

I have _____
_____

IMAGES of Goal and Achievement

Goal

VICTORY ☐ ACHIEVED

Rewards

Values Fulfilled by Achievement

Stated Goal

It is now

I feel

I am

I have

IMAGES of Goal and Achievement

Goal

VICTORY ☐ ACHIEVED

Rewards

Values Fulfilled by Achievement

Stated Goal

It is now

I feel

I am

I have

IMAGES of Goal and Achievement

Goal

VICTORY ☐ ACHIEVED

Rewards

Values Fulfilled by Achievement

Stated Goal

It is now _____

I feel _____
_____

I am _____
_____

I have _____
_____

IMAGES of Goal and Achievement

Goal

VICTORY ☐ **ACHIEVED**

Rewards

Values Fulfilled by Achievement

Stated Goal

It is now _____

I feel _____

I am _____

I have _____

IMAGES of Goal and Achievement

GOAL

VICTORY ☐ ACHIEVED

REWARDS

VALUES Fulfilled by Achievement

STATED GOAL

It is now _____

I feel _____

I am _____

I have _____

IMAGES of Goal and Achievement

Goal

VICTORY
☐
ACHIEVED

Rewards

Values Fulfilled by Achievement

Stated Goal

It is now _____

I feel _____
_____

I am _____
_____
_____

I have _____
_____

IMAGES of Goal and Achievement

Goal

VICTORY ☐ ACHIEVED

Rewards

Values Fulfilled by Achievement

Stated Goal

It is now

I feel

I am

I have

IMAGES of Goal and Achievement

Goal

VICTORY ☐ ACHIEVED

Rewards

Values Fulfilled by Achievement

Stated Goal

It is now

I feel

I am

I have

IMAGES of Goal and Achievement

Goal

☐ VICTORY ACHIEVED

Rewards

Values Fulfilled by Achievement

Stated Goal

It is now

I feel

I am

I have

IMAGES of Goal and Achievement

Goal

VICTORY ☐ ACHIEVED

Rewards

Values Fulfilled by Achievement

Stated Goal

It is now _____

I feel _____

I am _____

I have _____

IMAGES of Goal and Achievement

Goal

Victory ☐ Achieved

Rewards

Values Fulfilled by Achievement

Stated Goal

It is now ....

I feel ....
....

I am ....
....

I have ....
....

IMAGES of Goal and Achievement

Goal

VICTORY ☐ ACHIEVED

Rewards

Values Fulfilled by Achievement

Stated Goal

It is now

I feel

I am

I have

IMAGES of Goal and Achievement

Goal

VICTORY ☐ ACHIEVED

Rewards

Values Fulfilled by Achievement

Stated Goal

It is now _____

I feel _____

I am _____

I have _____

IMAGES of Goal and Achievement

Goal

VICTORY ☐ ACHIEVED

Rewards

Values Fulfilled by Achievement

Stated Goal

It is now

I feel

I am

I have

IMAGES of Goal and Achievement

Goal

VICTORY ☐ **ACHIEVED**

Rewards

Values Fulfilled by Achievement

Stated Goal

It is now

I feel

I am

I have

IMAGES of Goal and Achievement

Goal

VICTORY ☐ ACHIEVED

Rewards

Values Fulfilled by Achievement

Stated Goal

It is now

I feel

I am

I have

IMAGES of Goal and Achievement

Goal

VICTORY ☐ ACHIEVED

Rewards

Values Fulfilled by Achievement

Stated Goal

It is now _____

I feel _____

I am _____

I have _____

IMAGES of Goal and Achievement

Goal

VICTORY ☐ ACHIEVED

Rewards

Values Fulfilled by Achievement

Stated Goal

It is now

I feel

I am

I have

IMAGES of Goal and Achievement

Goal

VICTORY
☐
ACHIEVED

Rewards

Values Fulfilled by Achievement

Stated Goal

It is now

I feel

I am

I have

The Goals Journal: If it's here, it happens — Duane Alley

IMAGES of Goal and Achievement

Goal

VICTORY ☐ ACHIEVED

Rewards

Values Fulfilled by Achievement

Stated Goal

It is now

I feel

I am

I have

IMAGES of Goal and Achievement

Goal

VICTORY
☐
ACHIEVED

Rewards

Values Fulfilled by Achievement

Stated Goal

It is now _____

I feel _____
_____

I am _____
_____
_____

I have _____
_____

The Goals Journal: If it's here, it happens — Duane Alley

IMAGES of Goal and Achievement

Goal

> VICTORY ☐ ACHIEVED

Rewards

Values Fulfilled by Achievement

Stated Goal

It is now _____

I feel _____
_____

I am _____
_____
_____

I have _____
_____

IMAGES of Goal and Achievement

Goal

VICTORY ☐ ACHIEVED

Rewards

Values Fulfilled by Achievement

Stated Goal

It is now

I feel

I am

I have

IMAGES of Goal and Achievement

Goal

VICTORY
☐
ACHIEVED

Rewards

Values Fulfilled by Achievement

Stated Goal

It is now

I feel

I am

I have

IMAGES of Goal and Achievement

Goal

VICTORY ☐ **ACHIEVED**

Rewards

Values Fulfilled by Achievement

Stated Goal

It is now

I feel

I am

I have

IMAGES of Goal and Achievement

Goal

VICTORY ☐ ACHIEVED

Rewards

Values Fulfilled by Achievement

Stated Goal

It is now

I feel

I am

I have

IMAGES of Goal and Achievement

Goal

VICTORY ☐ ACHIEVED

Rewards

Values Fulfilled by Achievement

Stated Goal

It is now

I feel

I am

I have

IMAGES of Goal and Achievement

Goal

VICTORY
☐
ACHIEVED

Rewards

Values Fulfilled by Achievement

Stated Goal

It is now

I feel

I am

I have

IMAGES of Goal and Achievement

Goal

VICTORY ☐ ACHIEVED

Rewards

Values Fulfilled by Achievement

Stated Goal

It is now

I feel

I am

I have

IMAGES of Goal and Achievement

Goal

VICTORY ☐ **ACHIEVED**

Rewards

Values Fulfilled by Achievement

Stated Goal

It is now

I feel

I am

I have

IMAGES of Goal and Achievement

Goal

VICTORY
☐
ACHIEVED

Rewards

Values Fulfilled by Achievement

Stated Goal

It is now

I feel

I am

I have

IMAGES of Goal and Achievement

Goal

VICTORY ☐ ACHIEVED

Rewards

Values Fulfilled by Achievement

Stated Goal

It is now

I feel

I am

I have

IMAGES of Goal and Achievement

Goal

VICTORY ☐ **ACHIEVED**

Rewards

Values Fulfilled by Achievement

Stated Goal

It is now

I feel

I am

I have

IMAGES of Goal and Achievement

Goal

VICTORY ☐ ACHIEVED

Rewards

Values Fulfilled by Achievement

Stated Goal

It is now _____

I feel _____
_____

I am _____
_____
_____

I have _____
_____

IMAGES of Goal and Achievement

Goal

VICTORY ☐ ACHIEVED

Rewards

Values Fulfilled by Achievement

Stated Goal

It is now

I feel

I am

I have

IMAGES of Goal and Achievement

GOAL

VICTORY ☐ **ACHIEVED**

REWARDS

VALUES Fulfilled by Achievement

STATED GOAL

It is now

I feel

I am

I have

IMAGES of Goal and Achievement

Goal

VICTORY ☐ ACHIEVED

Rewards

Values Fulfilled by Achievement

Stated Goal

It is now

I feel

I am

I have

IMAGES of Goal and Achievement

GOAL

VICTORY ☐ ACHIEVED

REWARDS

VALUES Fulfilled by Achievement

STATED GOAL

It is now _____

I feel _____
_____

I am _____
_____

I have _____
_____

The Goals Journal: If it's here, it happens — Duane Alley

IMAGES of Goal and Achievement

GOAL

VICTORY ☐ ACHIEVED

REWARDS

VALUES Fulfilled by Achievement

STATED GOAL

It is now

I feel

I am

I have

IMAGES of Goal and Achievement

Goal

VICTORY ☐ ACHIEVED

Rewards

Values Fulfilled by Achievement

Stated Goal

It is now

I feel

I am

I have

The Goals Journal: If it's here, it happens — Duane Alley

IMAGES of Goal and Achievement

Goal

VICTORY ☐ ACHIEVED

Rewards

Values Fulfilled by Achievement

Stated Goal

It is now

I feel

I am

I have

IMAGES of Goal and Achievement

Goal

VICTORY ☐ ACHIEVED

Rewards

Values Fulfilled by Achievement

Stated Goal

It is now

I feel

I am

I have

IMAGES of Goal and Achievement

GOAL

VICTORY ☐ ACHIEVED

REWARDS

VALUES Fulfilled by Achievement

STATED GOAL

It is now _____

I feel _____
_____

I am _____
_____
_____

I have _____
_____

IMAGES of Goal and Achievement

Goal

VICTORY
☐
ACHIEVED

Rewards

Values Fulfilled by Achievement

Stated Goal

It is now

I feel

I am

I have

IMAGES of Goal and Achievement

Goal

VICTORY ☐ ACHIEVED

Rewards

Values Fulfilled by Achievement

Stated Goal

It is now

I feel

I am

I have

IMAGES of Goal and Achievement

Goal

VICTORY ☐ ACHIEVED

Rewards

Values Fulfilled by Achievement

Stated Goal

It is now

I feel

I am

I have

IMAGES of Goal and Achievement

Goal

VICTORY
☐
ACHIEVED

Rewards

Values Fulfilled by Achievement

Stated Goal

It is now _____

I feel _____
_____

I am _____
_____

I have _____
_____

IMAGES of Goal and Achievement

Goal

☐ VICTORY ACHIEVED

Rewards

Values Fulfilled by Achievement

Stated Goal

It is now

I feel

I am

I have

IMAGES of Goal and Achievement

GOAL

VICTORY ☐ ACHIEVED

REWARDS

VALUES Fulfilled by Achievement

STATED GOAL

It is now _____

I feel _____
_____

I am _____
_____
_____

I have _____
_____

IMAGES of Goal and Achievement

Goal

VICTORY
☐
ACHIEVED

Rewards

Values Fulfilled by Achievement

Stated Goal

It is now ....

I feel ....
....

I am ....
....

I have ....
....

IMAGES of Goal and Achievement

Goal

VICTORY ☐ ACHIEVED

Rewards

Values Fulfilled by Achievement

Stated Goal

It is now

I feel

I am

I have

IMAGES of Goal and Achievement

GOAL

VICTORY ☐ ACHIEVED

REWARDS

VALUES Fulfilled by Achievement

STATED GOAL

It is now _____

I feel _____

I am _____

I have _____

The Goals Journal: If it's here, it happens — Duane Alley

IMAGES of Goal and Achievement

Goal

VICTORY ☐ ACHIEVED

Rewards

Values Fulfilled by Achievement

Stated Goal

It is now

I feel

I am

I have

IMAGES of Goal and Achievement

Goal

VICTORY ☐ ACHIEVED

Rewards

Values Fulfilled by Achievement

Stated Goal

It is now

I feel

I am

I have

IMAGES of Goal and Achievement

| GOAL | VICTORY ☐ ACHIEVED |

REWARDS

VALUES Fulfilled by Achievement

STATED GOAL

It is now _____

I feel _____
_____

I am _____
_____

I have _____
_____

The Goals Journal: If it's here, it happens — Duane Alley

IMAGES of Goal and Achievement

Goal

VICTORY ☐ ACHIEVED

Rewards

Values Fulfilled by Achievement

Stated Goal

It is now _____

I feel _____

I am _____

I have _____

IMAGES of Goal and Achievement

| GOAL | VICTORY ☐ ACHIEVED |

REWARDS

VALUES Fulfilled by Achievement

STATED GOAL

It is now _____

I feel _____
_____

I am _____
_____
_____

I have _____
_____

IMAGES of Goal and Achievement

Goal

VICTORY ☐ ACHIEVED

Rewards

Values Fulfilled by Achievement

Stated Goal

It is now _____

I feel _____
_____

I am _____
_____
_____

I have _____
_____

IMAGES of Goal and Achievement

GOAL

VICTORY
☐
ACHIEVED

REWARDS

VALUES Fulfilled by Achievement

STATED GOAL

It is now

I feel

I am

I have

IMAGES of Goal and Achievement

GOAL

VICTORY
☐
ACHIEVED

REWARDS

VALUES Fulfilled by Achievement

STATED GOAL

It is now

I feel

I am

I have

IMAGES of Goal and Achievement

GOAL

VICTORY ☐ ACHIEVED

REWARDS

VALUES Fulfilled by Achievement

STATED GOAL

It is now

I feel

I am

I have

IMAGES of Goal and Achievement

Goal

VICTORY
☐
ACHIEVED

Rewards

Values Fulfilled by Achievement

Stated Goal

It is now

I feel

I am

I have

IMAGES of Goal and Achievement

Goal

VICTORY ☐ ACHIEVED

Rewards

Values Fulfilled by Achievement

Stated Goal

It is now

I feel

I am

I have

IMAGES of Goal and Achievement

Goal

VICTORY ☐ ACHIEVED

Rewards

Values Fulfilled by Achievement

Stated Goal

It is now _____

I feel _____

I am _____

I have _____

IMAGES of Goal and Achievement

Goal

Victory Achieved ☐

Rewards

Values Fulfilled by Achievement

Stated Goal

It is now

I feel

I am

I have

IMAGES of Goal and Achievement

Goal

VICTORY ☐ **ACHIEVED**

Rewards

Values Fulfilled by Achievement

Stated Goal

It is now

I feel

I am

I have

IMAGES of Goal and Achievement

Goal

☐ VICTORY ACHIEVED

Rewards

Values Fulfilled by Achievement

Stated Goal

It is now

I feel

I am

I have

IMAGES of Goal and Achievement

Goal

VICTORY
☐
ACHIEVED

Rewards

Values Fulfilled by Achievement

Stated Goal

It is now

I feel

I am

I have

IMAGES of Goal and Achievement

Goal

VICTORY ☐ ACHIEVED

Rewards

Values Fulfilled by Achievement

Stated Goal

It is now

I feel

I am

I have

The Goals Journal: If it's here, it happens — Duane Alley

IMAGES of Goal and Achievement

Goal

VICTORY ☐ **ACHIEVED**

Rewards

Values Fulfilled by Achievement

Stated Goal

It is now

I feel

I am

I have

IMAGES of Goal and Achievement

Goal

VICTORY ☐ ACHIEVED

Rewards

Values Fulfilled by Achievement

Stated Goal

It is now _____

I feel _____

I am _____

I have _____

IMAGES of Goal and Achievement

GOAL

☐ VICTORY ACHIEVED

REWARDS

VALUES Fulfilled by Achievement

STATED GOAL

It is now

I feel

I am

I have

The Goals Journal: If it's here, it happens — Duane Alley

IMAGES of Goal and Achievement

Goal

☐ VICTORY ACHIEVED

Rewards

Values Fulfilled by Achievement

Stated Goal

It is now

I feel

I am

I have

IMAGES of Goal and Achievement

Goal

VICTORY ☐ ACHIEVED

Rewards

Values Fulfilled by Achievement

Stated Goal

It is now

I feel

I am

I have

IMAGES of Goal and Achievement

Goal

VICTORY ☐ ACHIEVED

Rewards

Values Fulfilled by Achievement

Stated Goal

It is now

I feel

I am

I have

The Goals Journal: If it's here, it happens — Duane Alley

IMAGES of Goal and Achievement

Goal

VICTORY
☐
ACHIEVED

Rewards

Values Fulfilled by Achievement

Stated Goal

It is now

I feel

I am

I have

IMAGES of Goal and Achievement

Goal

VICTORY ☐ ACHIEVED

Rewards

Values Fulfilled by Achievement

Stated Goal

It is now

I feel

I am

I have

IMAGES of Goal and Achievement

Goal

☐ VICTORY ACHIEVED

Rewards

Values Fulfilled by Achievement

Stated Goal

It is now

I feel

I am

I have

IMAGES of Goal and Achievement

Goal

VICTORY
☐
ACHIEVED

Rewards

Values Fulfilled by Achievement

Stated Goal

It is now

I feel

I am

I have

IMAGES of Goal and Achievement

Goal

Victory ☐ Achieved

Rewards

Values Fulfilled by Achievement

Stated Goal

It is now

I feel

I am

I have

IMAGES of Goal and Achievement

Goal

VICTORY ☐ ACHIEVED

Rewards

Values Fulfilled by Achievement

Stated Goal

It is now

I feel

I am

I have

IMAGES of Goal and Achievement

Goal

VICTORY
☐
ACHIEVED

Rewards

Values Fulfilled by Achievement

Stated Goal

It is now

I feel

I am

I have

IMAGES of Goal and Achievement

GOAL

VICTORY
☐
ACHIEVED

REWARDS

VALUES Fulfilled by Achievement

STATED GOAL

It is now

I feel

I am

I have

IMAGES of Goal and Achievement

Goal

☐ VICTORY ACHIEVED

Rewards

Values Fulfilled by Achievement

Stated Goal

It is now

I feel

I am

I have

IMAGES of Goal and Achievement

Goal

VICTORY
☐
ACHIEVED

Rewards

Values Fulfilled by Achievement

Stated Goal

It is now

I feel

I am

I have

IMAGES of Goal and Achievement

Goal

VICTORY ☐ **ACHIEVED**

Rewards

Values Fulfilled by Achievement

Stated Goal

It is now _____

I feel _____

I am _____

I have _____

The Goals Journal: If it's here, it happens — Duane Alley

IMAGES of Goal and Achievement

Goal

VICTORY ☐ ACHIEVED

Rewards

Values Fulfilled by Achievement

Stated Goal

It is now

I feel

I am

I have

IMAGES of Goal and Achievement

Goal

VICTORY ☐ ACHIEVED

Rewards

Values Fulfilled by Achievement

Stated Goal

It is now

I feel

I am

I have

IMAGES of Goal and Achievement

GOAL

VICTORY
☐
ACHIEVED

REWARDS

VALUES Fulfilled by Achievement

STATED GOAL

It is now

I feel

I am

I have

IMAGES of Goal and Achievement

Goal

VICTORY
☐
ACHIEVED

Rewards

Values Fulfilled by Achievement

Stated Goal

It is now

I feel

I am

I have

IMAGES of Goal and Achievement

Goal

☐ VICTORY ACHIEVED

Rewards

Values Fulfilled by Achievement

Stated Goal

It is now

I feel

I am

I have

The Goals Journal: If it's here, it happens — Duane Alley

IMAGES of Goal and Achievement

Goal

VICTORY ☐ **ACHIEVED**

Rewards

Values Fulfilled by Achievement

Stated Goal

It is now _____

I feel _____

I am _____

I have _____

The Goals Journal: If it's here, it happens — Duane Alley

IMAGES of Goal and Achievement

Goal

VICTORY
☐
ACHIEVED

Rewards

Values Fulfilled by Achievement

Stated Goal

It is now ....

I feel ....
....

I am ....
....

I have ....
....

about the author
— DUANE ALLEY —

TRAINER | AUTHOR | SPEAKER | COACH

Duane Alley spent the first 15 years of his professional life working with some of the biggest and fastest growing retail and franchise businesses in the country; he then spent 5 years as Head Trainer & Coach for one of the biggest Personal Development companies on the planet.

He has combined his extensive experience from the business world in delivering real world results with his success and study of personal development, rapid human change and shifting consciousness.

As a Master Trainer, Author, Speaker and Performance Coach he now works with businesses and entrepreneurs quickly and easily improve their businesses and make more money and with individuals, couples and families to make simple changes and take small steps to live better lives day by day.

KEEP IN TOUCH:

 www.duanealley.com

www.facebook.com/duanealleypage

 www.twitter.com/DuaneAlley

 www.youtube.com/duanealley

 success@duanealley.com

FIND OUT
the BASIC HABITS THAT WINNERS USE ON A DAILY BASIS to CONSTANTLY IMPROVE THEIR LIVES!

In the latest in the *Seven Secrets series*, Duane Alley shows you seven habits that will get you connected with your goals, help you to keep focus on them, stay on the track to your target and resist every obstacle that tries to knock you off the path. The book also takes you through a number of interactive exercises that will help you to fine-tune the details and prepare you for the road to success.

Read this book and get the tools **to live your LIFE to its FULLEST!**

WHAT YOU WILL LEARN:

- ☑ Focussing solidly on your outcome
- ☑ Taking immediate strategic action
- ☑ Being fully aware and attentive
- ☑ An unstoppable ability to adapt
- ☑ Decision making super-powers

Join Master Trainer, Duane Alley, in his latest book and find out how you can immediately gain focus and take action from the minute you are awake to the time you are asleep. Soon, you will be on the path to achieving your goals, dreams and greatest desires.

VISIT DUANE ALLEY TRAINING ONLINE STORE:
www.DuaneAlley.com

Discover the
7 simple secrets
of how to have abundant energy in your day to day life so you can take on the world and **have everything you deserve!**

Have you ever wondered how some people just seem to overflow with energy and enthusiasm? Have you met people who always seem to be naturally "up" and "switched on" all the time, no matter how hard they play? Have you ever wanted to enjoy a level of energy that would allow you to do what you need to in life... and have ample left "in the tank" to do **EVERYTHING you WANT** as well?

Master Trainer, Duane Alley, is back with the second book in the *7 Secrets Series*. Discover the secrets to having incredible amounts of energy every day so you can truly create the life of your dreams and be able to enjoy it with those you love.

VISIT DUANE ALLEY TRAINING ONLINE STORE:
www.DuaneAlley.com

Discover
the simple secrets and small steps that together create **a new way** of **living better** day by day!

Most people focus so intently on the achievement of a goal or goals. What they forget or have never been taught is that the achievement of a goal is a fixed point in time. It is a single event that happens and once done is over.

What we truly desire to be focussed on is the creation of the life we want after we have achieved the goal. After all, the reason we achieved the goal was to have the life we get afterwards — make sense?

We get so hung up on "achievement" as the ultimate aim that we forego the real reward which is living an incredible life as we design it or choose it to be.

Join Master Trainer, Duane Alley, for 7 Minutes a Day and uncover a brand new way of focus and action so you can wake up every morning and plan every week to guarantee you are on path to achieving your goals, dreams and greatest desires.

VISIT DUANE ALLEY TRAINING ONLINE STORE:
www.DuaneAlley.com

GIFT OF GRATITUDE JOURNEY

PAPERBACK JOURNAL BOOK

The Gift of Gratitude is a one of the Powerful "Inner Games of Excellence" discussed in Duane Alley's Best Selling book *7 Secret Habits of Success*.

This book is a 6 month Journey to truly understanding and appreciating the incredible power of "Gratitude" in our lives.

As a structured journal and easy to follow and allow system of bringing Gratitude into our lives everyday, this book changes your live, love, living and ultimately the success you create around you everyday.

VISIT DUANE ALLEY TRAINING ONLINE STORE:
www.DuaneAlley.com

HOW TO STOP BURNOUT EBOOK

DIGITAL EBOOK

SIMPLE STEPS TO SURVIVE THE STRESSFUL SITUATIONS OF EVERYDAY LIFE.

Learn how to notice and fight the signs of burnout and the blues even before they take hold!

Get a copy of the book for yourself or a friend in need of guidance!

VISIT DUANE ALLEY TRAINING ONLINE STORE:

www.DuaneAlley.com

MAKE IT SIMPLE EBOOK

DIGITAL EBOOK

Around the world, millions of people struggle with stress, anxiety, or mood problems. These issues can wear and tear on your body and mind leaving you feeling tired, drained, and empty inside. Over time, stress and anxiety can build causing you to be less productive, anxious, tense, and very unhappy.

Is it possible to exist without stress? NO!

But stress, in and of itself, isn't bad. Confronting stress is a science and an art. If you prefer to live a happy and productive life, you have to learn how to more effectively deal with it.

Accompany me on this energising journey, which can bring a modification in your life, and determine how you too can make your life (negative-) stress free or with significantly less (bad-)stress.

VISIT DUANE ALLEY TRAINING ONLINE STORE:
www.DuaneAlley.com

BUSINESS BREAKTHROUGH BASICS EBOOK

DIGITAL EBOOK

BACK TO SCHOOL LESSONS FOR BUSINESS SUCCESS AT ANY LEVEL!

I wrote this Ebook to help you get your "stuff" together as a business person. When I'm working with many business people either in my live trainings or private coaching/consulting, the number of people who have missed the basics constantly surprises me. They've got all the fancy strategies and do-dads but the fundamentals are absent. It's like a school student returning to school without any books at all.

So take the time now to commit to sitting down and not only reading this Ebook – but learning from it and readying yourself to put the lessons to work or your business.

VISIT DUANE ALLEY TRAINING ONLINE STORE:
www.DuaneAlley.com

SUCCESS ALCHEMY EBOOK

....

DIGITAL EBOOK

Can you think of a successful business person who has not faced some kind of failure in their career?

Probably not; because there aren't any. Behind every business success, from Oprah Winfrey to Donald Trump is a string of not so successful events. What separated these people from becoming cautionary tales was their ability to bounce back from failure.

Through this Ebook I am going to share a series of 10 secrets of what I call 'Success Alchemy' that can help you turn your failures of any size and in any area of your life into successes. It's a transformative process that the most successful business people already know how to do, and I'm going to share their secrets with you.

Whether your first business failed, your latest product launch bombed, or you're on the brink of losing it all, there are lessons to be learnt and ways to recover.

VISIT DUANE ALLEY TRAINING ONLINE STORE:
www.DuaneAlley.com

— NOTES —

www.ingramcontent.com/pod-product-compliance
Lightning Source LLC
Chambersburg PA
CBHW030439300426
44112CB00009B/1076